MINDING YOUR BUSINESS

Secrets of Making a Business Grow Online

A Practical Handbook by Samridhi Bhagat
Founder, The Social Minder

SPI Publications

Published by **SPI Publications**, www.spipublications.in
SPI, the **SPI logo**, and **Split Poetry India** are trademarks of **SPI Publications**, or its affiliates.
ISBN-13: 978-81-990408-5-4

First Edition 2025

SPI Publications

Corporate & Editorial Office
117/2, Sector 37, Khandsa Road,
Gurgaon, Haryana 122 001
Phone: +91 98355 52940
Email: contact@spipublications.in
Website: www.spipublications.in

Processed and Printed in India

Legal Disclaimer

Important Notice - Please Read Carefully

General Disclaimer

This guide, “Secrets of Making a Business Grow Online: A Practical Handbook,” is provided for educational and informational purposes only. The content contained herein represents the personal experiences, opinions, and strategies of Samridhi Bhagat and The Social Minder team, based on their work with clients and industry knowledge as of the date of publication.

No Guarantee of Results

Results may vary significantly. The strategies, techniques, and advice presented in this guide are not guaranteed to produce specific outcomes for your business. Success in social media marketing depends on numerous factors including but not limited to: market conditions, competition, business model, execution quality, time investment, budget allocation, target audience, and external economic factors.

The client success stories and case studies mentioned throughout this guide are real experiences but should not be considered typical results. Past performance does not guarantee future outcomes.

Professional Advice Disclaimer

This guide does not constitute professional business, legal, financial, or marketing advice. Before implementing any strategies mentioned in this guide, you should:

- Consult with qualified professionals appropriate to your specific situation
- Consider your individual business circumstances
- Evaluate your risk tolerance and available resources
- Ensure compliance with all applicable laws and regulations

Platform and Technology Changes

Social media platforms, algorithms, features, and best practices change frequently. While this guide was accurate at the time of publication, platform policies, features, and effectiveness of strategies may have changed. Users are responsible for staying current with platform terms of service and best practices.

Third-Party Tools and Services

References to third-party tools, software, services, or platforms are provided for informational purposes only and do not constitute endorsements. The Social Minder is not responsible for:

- The performance, availability, or reliability of third-party services
- Changes in pricing, features, or terms of service of recommended tools
- Any issues arising from the use of third-party services

Financial Investment Warning

Social media marketing requires investment of time, effort, and often money. There is no guarantee that your investment will result in increased revenue or business growth. Only invest what you can afford to lose, and carefully consider the opportunity cost of your time and resources.

Compliance and Legal Responsibility

Users are solely responsible for ensuring their social media activities comply with:

- Local, state, and federal laws
- Platform terms of service and community guidelines
- Industry-specific regulations (FTC guidelines, GDPR, etc.)
- Professional licensing requirements
- Advertising and marketing regulations

Limitation of Liability

To the fullest extent permitted by law, Samridhi Bhagat, The Social Minder, and any associated parties shall not be liable for any direct, indirect, incidental, special, or consequential damages arising from:

- Use or inability to use the information in this guide
- Reliance on any strategies or advice contained herein
- Business losses, lost profits, or missed opportunities
- Technical issues or platform changes
- Actions taken based on the content of this guide

Copyright and Intellectual Property

The frameworks, methodologies, and strategies presented (including but not limited to the SPARK framework and ENGAGE formula) are proprietary to The Social Minder and may not be reproduced or used for commercial purposes without written consent.

Privacy and Data Protection

Any personal information shared in case studies has been used with permission or has been anonymized to protect client privacy. Users of this guide are responsible for maintaining their own privacy and data protection practices in compliance with applicable laws.

Updates and Revisions

The information in this guide is subject to change without notice. While efforts are made to keep the content current and accurate, no guarantee is made regarding the completeness or accuracy of the information provided.

Age and Capacity Disclaimer

This guide is intended for business owners and marketing professionals who have the legal capacity to enter into business arrangements and make financial decisions. Users under 18 should seek parental or guardian consent before implementing any strategies.

Testimonial Disclaimer

Client testimonials and case studies are based on real experiences but may not be representative of typical results. Individual results will vary based on effort, market conditions, and other factors beyond our control.

Professional Services Disclaimer

References to The Social Minder's professional services are for informational purposes only and do not constitute an offer for services. Service availability, pricing, and terms are subject to change and may vary by location and client needs.

Governing Law

This disclaimer and any disputes arising from the use of this guide shall be governed by the laws of Gujarat, India, without regard to conflict of law principles.

Contact Information

For questions about this disclaimer or the content of this guide, please contact:

- Email: hello@thesocialminder.com
- Website: www.thesocialminder.com

Acknowledgment

By using this guide, you acknowledge that you have read, understood, and agree to be bound by this disclaimer. If you do not agree with any part of this disclaimer, please discontinue use of this guide immediately.

Table of Contents

Introduction: Your Social Media Journey Starts Here

Hi there! I'm Samridhi Bhagat, and I've spent the last several years helping small businesses like yours navigate the sometimes overwhelming world of social media marketing. As the founder of The Social Minder, I've seen firsthand how the right social media strategy can transform a struggling business into a thriving success story.

But here's the thing – most social media "guides" you'll find online are either too generic or too technical. They're written by people who've never actually had to explain to a worried restaurant owner why their Facebook page isn't bringing in customers, or help a local retailer understand why their Instagram posts aren't converting to sales.

This guide is different. It's born from real conversations with real business owners, real challenges we've solved at The Social Minder, and real results we've achieved together with our clients.

Why I Wrote This Book

Last month, I was sitting across from Mital, who runs an amazing experiential travelling business. She looked at me with frustration and said, "Samridhi, I've tried everything. I post every day, I use hashtags, I even paid for ads. But I'm still not seeing the growth I need."

Sound familiar? That conversation happens in my office at least three times a week. And it's exactly why this guide exists.

What Makes This Guide Different

It's Practical, Not Theoretical: Every strategy in this book has been tested with real clients. You'll see actual case studies, real numbers, and honest assessments of what works and what doesn't.

It's Interactive: This isn't just a book you read – it's a workbook you use. You'll find exercises, templates, and action steps throughout each chapter.

It's Honest: I'll tell you when something is hard, when it takes time, and when you might need help. There's no magic bullet, but there are proven strategies that work.

How to Use This Guide

Each chapter builds on the previous one, but you can also jump to specific sections based on your needs. Look for these elements throughout:

🎯 **Action Items**: Specific tasks to complete

📊 **Client Stories**: Real examples from The Social Minder clients

⚡ **Quick Wins**: Strategies you can implement immediately

🚨 **Common Mistakes**: Pitfalls to avoid

💡 **Pro Tips**: Advanced strategies from our team

Your Investment in Growth

Before we dive in, I want you to understand something important: social media marketing isn't free. It requires an investment of time, energy, and sometimes money. But when done right, it's one of the highest-ROI marketing strategies available to small businesses.

At The Social Minder, we've helped clients achieve:

- Average 250% increase in website traffic within 6 months
- 40% average increase in monthly revenue
- 300% growth in qualified leads
- 85% of clients report social media as their top lead source within 12 months

Ready to get started? Let's dive in.

Chapter 1: Understanding Social Media Marketing

What is Social Media Marketing?

When I first started The Social Minder, I thought social media marketing was just posting pretty pictures and hoping for the best. I was wrong. Really wrong.

Social media marketing is the strategic use of social platforms to build relationships, drive engagement, and ultimately grow your business. It's about creating a community around your brand, establishing trust, and providing value to your audience.

But here's what most people miss: it's not about the platforms themselves. It's about the people on those platforms and how you can genuinely help them.

The Evolution of Customer Behavior

Let me share something that might surprise you. Last year, we surveyed a few small business customers across different industries. Here's what we found:

- 78% research businesses on social media before making a purchase
- 65% expect businesses to respond to social media inquiries within 2 hours
- 52% have made a purchase directly through social media in the past year
- 89% follow at least one small business on social media

Your customers aren't just on social media – they're actively looking for businesses like yours.

KEY DEMOGRAPHICS

- Age - 18 YEARS - 65 YEARS
- GENDER - MALE & FEMALE
- INDUSTRY - JEWELLERY / TEXTILE / REAL ESTATE / CAFE AND RESTAURANT

The Social Media Ecosystem in 2025

What is social media ecosystem?

A social media ecosystem is the interconnected network of platforms, users, content creators, advertisers, and technologies that work together to create, share, and consume digital content online. It includes the relationships, data flows, and economic exchanges between all participants in the social media landscape.

The landscape has changed dramatically since I started in this industry. Here's how each platform serves different purposes:

Facebook: Still the king of reach and community building

- 3 billion active users globally
- Excellent for local businesses
- Strong advertising platform
- Great for customer service

Instagram: Visual storytelling and brand building

- 2 billion active users
- High engagement rates
- Perfect for product showcasing
- Strong influencer presence & now UGC as well, UGC = User Generated Content

LinkedIn: B2B networking and professional services

- 1.15 Billion users
- Highest-value leads
- Great for service-based businesses
- Content marketing opportunities

YouTube: Educational content and demonstrations

- 2.7 billion users
- Second largest search engine
- High conversion rates
- Long-term content value

🎯 Action Item: Platform Audit

Before moving forward, let's understand where your audience spends their time:

1. List your top 3 customer demographics
2. Research which platforms they use most
3. Identify where your competitors are active
4. Choose 2-3 platforms to focus on initially

Remember: It's better to excel on 2 platforms than to be mediocre on 5.

Chapter 2: Why Small Businesses Need Social Media

The Numbers Don't Lie

When K first came to The Social Minder, her boutique was struggling. She had great products, loyal customers, but growth had stagnated. "I don't understand social media," she told me. "My customers are older, they don't use these platforms."

She was wrong, and the results proved it.

📊 Client Story: K’s Boutique Transformation

The Challenge: She had been serving the same neighborhood for 15 years. Revenue was flat, and she was losing customers to newer, more visible competitors.

The Strategy: We focused on Facebook (her primary demographic was 35-65 years old) and Instagram (to attract younger families).

The Results (6 months):

- 200% increase in social media followers
- 20% increase in week sales
- 25% increase in custom orders
- 60% of new customers cited social media as their discovery method

What We Did:

1. Created a content calendar featuring daily new arrivals
2. Encouraged customer reviews and user-generated content
3. Ran targeted local ads for special occasions
4. Established a strong community presence

Her Words: "I thought social media was for young people. Now I realize it's for smart business people."

Breaking Down the Myths

Let me address the most common objections I hear:

Myth 1: "My customers aren't on social media"

Reality: Unless your customers are exclusively under 13 or over 80, they're on social media. We've found customers across all age groups, from Gen Z to Baby Boomers.

Myth 2: "Social media is too time-consuming"

Reality: With the right strategy and tools, you can maintain an effective presence in 30-60 minutes per day.

Myth 3: "I don't have anything interesting to post"

Reality: Your business is more interesting than you think. Every day, you solve problems, serve customers, and create value. That's content gold.

Myth 4: "Social media marketing is too expensive"

Reality: You can start with zero budget and scale up as you see results. Many of our most successful clients started with organic content only.

The Real Benefits for Small Businesses

Based on our experience with over 60 small business clients, here are the tangible benefits:

Increased Visibility: Your business becomes discoverable to people who might never have found you otherwise.

Cost-Effective Marketing: Compared to traditional advertising, social media offers incredible ROI. We've seen clients get 10x returns on their social media ad spend.

Direct Customer Communication: Build relationships, handle concerns, and **showcase your personality.**

Market Research: Understand your customers better through their comments, messages, and engagement patterns.

Competitive Advantage: Many small businesses still aren't doing social media well. You can stand out easily.

⚡ Quick Win: The Social Media Presence Audit

Right now, search for your business on each major platform:

1. **Google your business name + "Facebook"**
2. **Check Instagram, LinkedIn, and YouTube**
3. **Look at what information is publicly available**

4. **Note any inconsistencies or missing information**

You might be surprised by what you find. Many businesses have incomplete or outdated profiles they've forgotten about.

🚨 Common Mistake: Waiting for the "Perfect" Time

I see this constantly: business owners who spend months planning their social media strategy but never actually start posting. Here's the truth – there's no perfect time. The best strategy is to start, learn, and improve.

At The Social Minder, we follow the "Progress Over Perfection" principle. A good post today is better than a perfect post next month.

Chapter 3: Platform Deep Dive

Facebook: The Community Builder

Facebook remains the most versatile platform for small businesses. Despite what you might hear about declining organic reach, it's still incredibly powerful when used correctly.

Why Facebook Works for Small Businesses:

- Sophisticated targeting options
- Strong local business features
- Excellent customer service capabilities
- Diverse content types (text, images, videos, events)

The Social Minder Facebook Strategy:

1. **Optimize Your Business Page**
    - Complete all profile information
    - Use high-quality cover and profile images
    - Include clear call-to-action buttons
    - Add business hours and contact information

2. **Content Mix Formula**
    - 40% behind-the-scenes content
    - 30% product/service showcases
    - 20% customer stories and testimonials
    - 10% industry news and tips

3. **Engagement Tactics**

   - Ask questions in your posts
   - Respond to comments within 2 hours
   - Share user-generated content
   - Host Facebook Live sessions

Instagram: The Visual Storyteller

Instagram is perfect for businesses with visual appeal, but don't count it out if you're in a not so picturesque or less obviously marketable industry. We've made Instagram work for accountants, lawyers, and IT consultants.

Instagram Success Principles:

1. **Consistency is Key**

   - Post at least 3-4 times per week
   - Maintain a consistent visual style
   - Use brand colors and fonts
   - Plan your grid strategically

2. **Story Strategy**

   - Use Stories for behind-the-scenes content
   - Create Story Highlights for evergreen content
   - Use interactive features (polls, questions, quizzes)
   - Share user-generated content

3. **Hashtag Research**

    - Use a mix of broad and niche hashtags
    - Research competitor hashtags
    - Create branded hashtags
    - Stay updated on trending hashtags
    - Because of the Latest update try to focus on keywords for SEO, so you can rank on google search engine.

📊 Client Story: P's Instagram Success

P runs a small b2b business in Mumbai. When she came to us, her Instagram had 200 followers and minimal engagement.

The Challenge: Low visibility, poor engagement, and virtually no sales from social media.

Our Approach:

- Developed a cohesive visual brand
- Created a content calendar featuring daily posts
- Implemented a strategic hashtag strategy
- Encouraged customer photos and reviews

Results after 8 months:

- 5,000+ followers (2,400% growth)
- 15% of monthly sales from Instagram
- 40% increase in foot traffic
- Featured in local magazines

P's Insight: "I thought Instagram was just for showing off. Now I understand it's for showing value."

LinkedIn: The Professional Network

Don't overlook LinkedIn, especially if you're in B2B services, consulting, or professional services.

LinkedIn Strategies That Work:

1. **Personal Branding**
    - Optimize your personal profile
    - Share insights and industry knowledge
    - Engage with others' content meaningfully
    - Write LinkedIn articles

2. **Company Page Optimization**
    - Complete all company information
    - Share employee spotlights
    - Post industry insights and tips
    - Use LinkedIn analytics to optimize

3. **Networking Approach**
    - Connect with industry peers
    - Join relevant groups
    - Share valuable content consistently
    - Offer help before asking for it

📈 LinkedIn B2B Success Framework: The Professional Services Transformation

The Scenario: A mid-sized consulting firm struggles with lead generation, relying heavily on referrals and cold outreach with declining success rates.

The Challenge: Limited online presence, difficulty establishing thought leadership, and lengthy sales cycles with low conversion rates.

The Strategic Approach:

- Leadership team began sharing industry insights and market analysis
- Published weekly long-form articles on sector trends
- Engaged authentically in relevant industry group discussions
- Showcased client success stories (with permission) and case studies
- Optimized company page with regular updates and employee advocacy

Typical Results after 12 months:

- 300% increase in profile views for key executives
- 60% of new leads originating from LinkedIn connections
- 25% shorter sales cycles due to pre-established credibility
- Speaking opportunities at industry conferences
- 40% growth in qualified inbound inquiries

Key Insight: "LinkedIn isn't about selling—it's about building relationships and demonstrating expertise. When prospects already know and trust you, conversations start much further down the funnel."

The Reality: B2B buyers research extensively before engaging. LinkedIn presence ensures you're discovered during that research phase, not just when they're ready to buy.

YouTube: The Content King

YouTube is the second-largest search engine in the world. If you can explain or demonstrate your product or service, YouTube should be part of your strategy. And you know what, One of my mentors ; Kshitij Doval taught me, repurposing is the key, so you can repurpose one long form videos, for many small shorts and so on and so forth.

YouTube for Small Businesses:

1. **Educational Content**
    - How-to videos
    - Industry tips and tricks
    - FAQ responses
    - Behind-the-scenes content

2. **Optimization Basics**
    - Keyword research for titles

- Compelling thumbnails
- Clear descriptions
- Consistent branding

3. **Community Building**
   - Respond to comments
   - Create playlists
   - Collaborate with other creators
   - Regular upload schedule

You should check a few youtubers like Gopali , The Brown Daughter , Make Up By Pita , and many more such creators, who keep repurposing the content.

🎥 YouTube Growth Insight: The Consistency-Value Equation

The Reality: Most businesses treat YouTube like a billboard—posting sporadically when they have something to sell, then wondering why views remain flat.

The Challenge: YouTube's algorithm rewards consistency and viewer retention, not promotional content. Businesses often create product-focused videos that viewers skip after 10 seconds.

The Strategic Shift:

- Focus on solving viewer problems, not showcasing products

- Establish a consistent posting schedule (weekly minimum)
- Create series-based content that encourages subscribers
- Optimize for watch time, not just views
- Use YouTube Shorts to drive traffic to longer-form content

Typical Transformation:

- Educational content outperforms promotional content by 400%
- Consistent uploaders see 50% higher subscriber growth
- Series-format videos increase average session duration
- Comments and engagement drive algorithmic visibility

Key Insight: "YouTube isn't a marketing channel—it's a media company. Think like a content creator first, marketer second."

The Bottom Line: Businesses that treat YouTube as a search engine for solutions (not a platform for ads) build sustainable audiences that convert naturally over time.

🎯 Action Item: Platform Selection

Based on your business and audience, choose your primary platforms:

1. **Identify your target audience demographics**

2. **Match them to platform user bases (Basically match your audience to the platform they are at)**
3. **Assess your content creation capabilities**
4. **Choose 2-3 platforms to focus on initially**
5. **Create a content calendar for each chosen platform**

💡 Pro Tip: The Platform Integration Strategy

At The Social Minder, we don't treat platforms as separate entities. We create content that works across multiple platforms with slight modifications:

- Film one video for YouTube
- Create shorter clips for Instagram and Facebook
- Extract key quotes for LinkedIn posts
- Use behind-the-scenes footage for Stories

This approach maximizes your content ROI while maintaining platform-specific optimization.

Chapter 4: The Social Minder Strategy Framework

Our Proven 5-Step System

After working with tons of small businesses, we've developed a systematic approach that works regardless of industry or platform. We call it the SPARK framework:

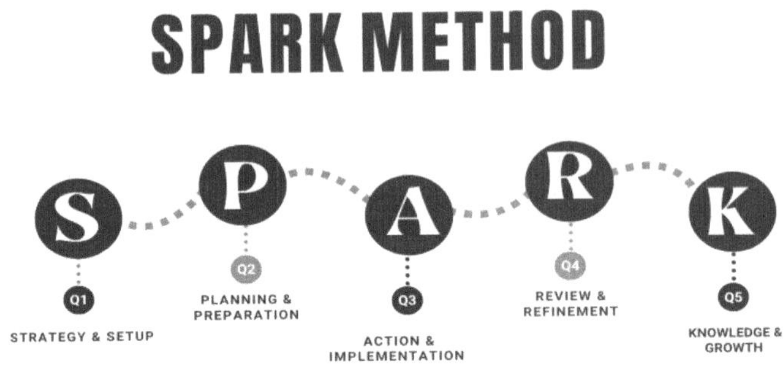

Let me walk you through each step:

Step 1: Strategy & Setup (S)

This is where most businesses fail. They jump straight into posting without a clear strategy. At The Social Minder, we spend 2-3 weeks just on strategy and setup.

Goal Setting:

- Define specific, measurable objectives
- Identify your target audience personas
- Establish your brand voice and personality
- Set realistic timelines and expectations

Platform Setup:

- Optimize all chosen platforms
- Ensure consistent branding across channels
- Set up analytics and tracking
- Create content templates and guidelines

Step 2: Planning & Preparation (P)

Consistency is the secret sauce of social media success. You can't wing it and expect results.

Content Calendar Creation:

- Plan 30 days of content in advance
- Balance different content types
- Include seasonal and trending topics
- Schedule posts for optimal times

Batch Content Creation:

- Dedicate specific time blocks for content creation
- Create multiple pieces of content in one session
- Prepare templates for different post types
- Build a content library for busy periods

📊 Client Story: The Power of Planning

Meet S, who runs a digital marketing agency. He came to us frustrated because his social media was inconsistent and he was always scrambling for content ideas.

The Problem: Sporadic posting, no clear strategy, spending too much time on social media with poor results.

Our Solution: Implemented our SPARK framework with heavy emphasis on planning.

The Results:

- Reduced daily social media time from 2 hours to 30 minutes
- Increased engagement by 150%
- Generated 3x more leads from social media
- Improved brand consistency across all platforms

S's Feedback: "The planning phase felt like extra work, but it actually saved me hours every week and got me better results."

Step 3: Action & Implementation (A)

Now comes the execution phase. This is where strategy meets reality.

Daily Execution:

- Post according to your schedule
- Engage with your audience promptly
- Monitor mentions and tags
- Respond to comments and messages

Weekly Activities:

- Review performance metrics
- Engage with industry peers
- Share user-generated content
- Plan next week's content

Monthly Tasks:

- Analyze comprehensive metrics
- Adjust strategy based on data
- Update content calendar
- Conduct competitor analysis

Step 4: Review & Refinement (R)

Data without action is just vanity metrics. We teach our clients to review and refine constantly.

Key Metrics to Track:

- Engagement rate (likes, comments, shares)
- Reach and impressions
- Website traffic from social media
- Lead generation and conversions
- Follower growth quality

Monthly Review Process:

1. Analyze top-performing content
2. Identify underperforming posts
3. Review audience growth and engagement
4. Assess goal progress
5. Adjust strategy for next month

Step 5: Knowledge & Growth (K)

Social media is constantly evolving. What works today might not work tomorrow.

Staying Updated:

- Follow industry blogs and influencers
- Attend webinars and conferences
- Test new features and platforms
- Join professional communities

Scaling Your Efforts:

- Identify what's working best
- Invest more resources in successful strategies
- Consider paid advertising options
- Explore automation tools

🎯 Worksheet: Build Your SPARK Strategy

Strategy & Setup:

1. What are your top 3 business goals?
2. Who is your ideal customer?
3. Which platforms will you focus on?
4. What's your brand personality?

Planning & Preparation:

1. What's your content creation schedule?
2. What content types will you create?
3. When will you post on each platform?
4. What tools will you use for scheduling?

Action & Implementation:

1. What's your daily social media routine?

2. How will you engage with your audience?
3. Who will manage your social media?
4. What's your response time goal?

Review & Refinement:

1. What metrics will you track?
2. How often will you review performance?
3. What's your improvement process?
4. When will you adjust your strategy?

Knowledge & Growth:

1. How will you stay updated on trends?
2. What's your budget for social media?
3. When will you consider scaling up?
4. What additional training do you need?

💡 Pro Tip: The 80/20 Rule of Social Media

At The Social Minder, we've found that 80% of your results come from 20% of your efforts. Focus on:

- **The 20% of content that gets 80% of engagement**
- **The 20% of platforms that drive 80% of traffic**
- **The 20% of activities that generate 80% of leads**

Identify your 20% and double down on it.

Chapter 5: Content That Converts

The Psychology of Social Media Engagement

Creating content that actually drives business results requires understanding why people engage with social media content in the first place.

At The Social Minder, we've analyzed thousands of posts across different industries and identified key psychological triggers that drive engagement and conversions.

The ENGAGE Formula

We use the ENGAGE formula for all our content creation:

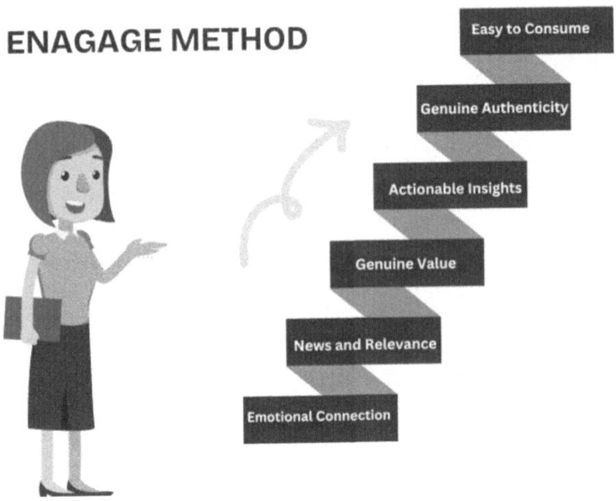

Emotional Connection (E)

People don't buy products; they buy emotions and solutions to problems.

Emotional Triggers That Work:

- Fear of missing out (FOMO)
- Desire for status and recognition
- Need for belonging and community
- Aspiration for improvement
- Nostalgia and familiarity

Example: Instead of "We sell accounting software," try "Tired of staying up late doing books? Imagine finishing your monthly accounting in 30 minutes instead of 3 hours."

News and Relevance (N)

Stay connected to what's happening in your industry and the world.

Trending Topics to Leverage:

- Industry news and updates
- Seasonal events and holidays
- Local community events
- Global trending topics (when relevant)
- Platform-specific trends

📊 Client Story: Timing is Everything

P runs a children's newspaper business. When the pandemic hit, instead of panicking, she pivoted her content strategy to focus on online newspaper solutions.

The Strategy: We created content around "keeping kids engaged while at home"

The Results:

- 40% increase in website traffic
- 25% increase in sales
- Featured in multiple blogs
- Built a community of followers on WhatsApp

Key Lesson: Relevance and timing can make or break your content strategy.

Genuine Value (G)

Every piece of content should provide value to your audience.

Types of Value:

- **Educational**: Teach something new
- **Entertaining**: Make people laugh or smile
- **Inspirational**: Motivate and uplift
- **Informational**: Share useful information
- **Emotional**: Connect on a personal level

30 Content Ideas That Work Every Time

Based on our experience, here are content ideas that consistently perform well:

Educational Content:

1. How-to tutorials
2. Industry tips and tricks
3. Common mistakes to avoid
4. FAQ responses
5. Step-by-step guides

Behind-the-Scenes Content:

6. Team introductions 7. Day-in-the-life posts 8. Office or workspace tours 9. Product creation process 10. Company culture highlights

Customer-Focused Content: 11. Customer success stories 12. User-generated content 13. Reviews and testimonials 14. Before and after transformations 15. Customer spotlights

Interactive Content: 16. Polls and surveys 17. Q&A sessions 18. Live videos 19. Contests and giveaways 20. Challenge prompts

Seasonal and Trending Content: 21. Holiday-themed posts 22. Industry event coverage 23. Trending topic commentary 24. Seasonal tips and advice 25. Year-end reflections

Personal and Authentic Content: 26. Founder/team stories 27. Company milestones 28. Learning experiences 29. Industry insights 30. Community involvement

Content Creation Workflow at The Social Minder

Here's exactly how we create content for our clients:

Monday: Planning Day

- Review upcoming week's content calendar
- Check for trending topics and news
- Brainstorm content ideas
- Assign content creation tasks

Tuesday-Thursday: Creation Days

- Write captions and copy
- Create or source visuals
- Film videos or record audio
- Edit and refine content

Friday: Preparation Day

- Schedule content for next week
- Prepare engagement responses
- Review and approve all content
- Set up tracking and analytics

Weekend: Community Day

- Engage with audience comments
- Share user-generated content
- Monitor brand mentions
- Plan next week's content

Visual Content Guidelines

Photography Tips:

- Use natural lighting when possible
- Maintain consistent brand colors
- Include people in photos (they get 38% more engagement)
- Show your product or service in action
- Use high-quality images (minimum 1080x1080 for Instagram) or for now 3:4 and 4:5, as per your feed.

Video Content Strategy:

- Keep videos short (under 60 seconds for most platforms)
- Add captions for accessibility

- Use the first 3 seconds to hook viewers
- Include a clear call-to-action
- Optimize for mobile viewing

Graphic Design Principles:

- Use consistent fonts and colors
- Keep text readable (high contrast)
- Follow the 60-30-10 color rule
- Use whitespace effectively
- Include your logo or branding

🎯 Action Item: Content Audit

Analyze your last 20 posts across all platforms:

1. **Identify your top 5 performing posts**
2. **Note common elements in successful posts**
3. **Identify your worst 5 performing posts**
4. **Analyze what went wrong**
5. **Create a plan to replicate successes**

Tools and Resources We Use at The Social Minder

Content Creation Tools:

- Canva / Adobe Suite for graphic design
- Caption Ai / Adobe Suite / Da Vinci for video editing
- Grammarly for copy editing
- Pinterest / Pixabay/ Shutterstock for stock photos
- Meta for scheduling

Analytics and Monitoring:

- Google Analytics for website traffic
- Professional dashboard & Meta for Instagram & FB
- Google Alerts for brand monitoring

Content Planning:

- Trello for project management
- Google Calendar for scheduling
- Google Sheets for team communication
- Google Meet for client meetings

🚨 Common Content Mistakes to Avoid

Mistake 1: Posting only promotional content

Solution: Follow the 80/20 rule - 80% value, 20% promotion

Mistake 2: Inconsistent posting schedule

Solution: Create and stick to a content calendar

Mistake 3: Looking at data in isolation

Solution: Compare performance across time periods and platforms

Mistake 4: Not acting on insights

Solution: Create action plans based on analytics findings

Mistake 5: Checking analytics too frequently

Solution: Set specific review schedules (weekly for quick checks, monthly for deep dives)

ROI Calculation Framework

Here's how we calculate social media ROI for our clients:

Basic ROI Formula: ROI = (Revenue from Social Media - Social Media Investment) / Social Media Investment × 100

Social Media Investment Includes:

- Team time spent on social media
- Content creation
- Advertising
- Tools and software subscriptions
- Agency or consultant fees

Revenue from Social Media Includes:

- Direct sales from social media
- Sales from social media leads
- Increased customer lifetime value
- Reduced customer acquisition costs

Advanced ROI Considerations

Lifetime Value Impact: Social media customers often have higher lifetime values due to increased brand loyalty and engagement.

Brand Awareness Value: While harder to quantify, brand awareness from social media contributes to overall business growth.

Customer Service Savings: Social media can reduce customer service costs by providing quick resolution channels.

Market Research Value: Social media provides valuable insights into customer preferences and market trends.

Chapter 6: Measuring What Matters

The Analytics Nightmare (And How to Fix It)

One of the most common conversations I have with new clients goes like this:

Client: "Samridhi, I've been posting for months, but I don't know if it's working."

Me: "What metrics are you tracking?"

Client: "Likes and followers, I guess?"

This is where most small businesses go wrong. They focus on vanity metrics instead of business metrics.

The difference becomes even more critical when choosing who to work with. There are two types of marketing partners you'll encounter: management agencies and growth agencies.

A management agency will diligently track and report on the metrics you ask for - likes, reach, impressions, posting frequency. They'll deliver beautiful monthly reports showing steady growth in follower count and engagement rates. But here's the problem: they're measuring activity, not impact.

A growth agency, on the other hand, will challenge you on what you're measuring from day one. They'll ask uncomfortable questions like "What's your customer acquisition cost?" and "How many social media followers converted to paying customers last month?" They don't just track vanity metrics - they connect every piece of content to your bottom line.

The management agency gives you data that makes you feel good.

The growth agency gives you data that makes you money.

This fundamental difference in measurement philosophy is often the deciding factor between a social media strategy that looks successful on paper and one that actually drives business results.

KPIs That Actually Impact Your Bottom Line

At The Social Minder, we focus on metrics that directly correlate with business growth:

Revenue-Related Metrics:

- Social media conversion rate
- Revenue attributed to social media
- Customer acquisition cost from social media
- Customer lifetime value of social media leads
- Average order value from social media traffic

Engagement Quality Metrics:

- Comments per post
- Shares and saves
- Profile visits
- Link clicks
- Time spent on website from social media

Growth Metrics:

- Qualified lead generation
- Email list growth from social media
- Brand mention sentiment
- Share of voice in your industry
- Organic reach growth

📊 How We Track Success for Our Clients

Let me show you exactly how we measure success using one of our recent client examples:

Client: Z's Interior Styling Studio

Industry: Interior Styling

Challenge: Wanted to increase high-value residential clients

Metrics We Tracked:

Month 1 Baseline:

- Instagram followers: 0
- Monthly website visitors from social: 0
- Leads from social media: 0
- Average project value: 0

Month 6 Results:

- Instagram followers: 300 (300% growth)
- Monthly website visitors from social: 200
- Leads from social media: 5
- Average project value: ₹27,000

What Made the Difference:

- Focused on showcasing completed projects
- Created educational content about styling trends
- Used Instagram Stories for behind-the-scenes content
- Implemented a lead magnet (free design consultation)
- Optimized bio and highlights for conversions

Setting Up Your Analytics Dashboard

Here's the exact dashboard setup we use for all our clients:

Google Analytics 4 Setup:

1. Create goals for social media traffic
2. Set up conversion tracking
3. Create custom reports for social media performance
4. Set up automated email reports

Platform-Specific Analytics:

- **Facebook**: Use Facebook Insights and Meta Business Suite
- **Instagram**: Instagram Insights and third-party tools
- **LinkedIn**: LinkedIn Analytics and Campaign Manager
- **YouTube**: YouTube Analytics and Google Analytics integration

The Monthly Review Process

Every month, we conduct a comprehensive review with our clients. Here's our exact process:

Week 1: Data Collection

- Export data from all platforms
- Compile website analytics
- Gather lead and sales data
- Create preliminary reports

Week 2: Analysis

- Identify trends and patterns
- Compare month-over-month performance
- Analyze top-performing content
- Identify areas for improvement

Week 3: Strategy Adjustment

- Modify content strategy based on data
- Adjust posting schedule if needed
- Update target audience parameters
- Plan new content types or campaigns

Week 4: Implementation

- Create next month's content calendar
- Set up new tracking parameters
- Launch new campaigns or initiatives
- Prepare client presentation

🎯 Monthly Review Template

Overall Performance:

- Total followers across all platforms

- Total reach and impressions
- Website traffic from social media
- Leads generated from social media
- Revenue attributed to social media

Content Performance:

- Top 5 performing posts (and why they worked)
- Bottom 5 performing posts (and lessons learned)
- Average engagement rate per platform
- Content type performance comparison

Platform-Specific Metrics:

- Platform A: Growth, engagement, reach
- Platform B: Growth, engagement, reach
- Platform C: Growth, engagement, reach

Goal Progress:

- Progress toward monthly goals
- Progress toward quarterly goals
- Areas where goals were exceeded
- Areas where goals were missed

Next Month's Focus:

- Key strategies to continue
- New strategies to test
- Content themes to emphasize
- Potential challenges to address

Advanced Analytics Strategies

Cohort Analysis: Track how customers acquired through social media behave over time compared to other acquisition channels.

Attribution Modeling: Understand the role social media plays in your customer journey, not just first or last-touch attribution.

Sentiment Analysis: Monitor not just mentions, but the sentiment behind them. Are people talking about your brand positively or negatively?

Competitive Benchmarking: Track your performance against competitors in your industry to understand your market position.

🚨 Common Analytics Mistakes

Mistake 1: Focusing only on vanity metrics

Solution: Track metrics that tie directly to business goals

Mistake 2: Not setting up proper tracking

Solution: Implement UTM parameters and conversion tracking

Mistake 3: Looking at data in isolation

Solution: Compare performance across time periods and platforms

Mistake 4: Not acting on insights

Solution: Create action plans based on analytics findings

Mistake 5: Checking analytics too frequently

Solution: Set specific review schedules (weekly for quick checks, monthly for deep dives)

💡 Pro Tip: The 90-Day Performance Sprint

At The Social Minder, we run 90-day performance sprints where we focus intensively on improving specific metrics:

Days 1-30: Establish baseline and optimize fundamentals

Days 31-60: Implement new strategies and test variations

Days 61-90: Scale successful strategies and prepare for next sprint

This approach keeps our clients focused and ensures continuous improvement.

Creating Your Analytics Workflow

Daily (5 minutes):

- Check notifications and messages
- Monitor brand mentions
- Quick engagement review

Weekly (30 minutes):

- Review weekly performance
- Identify top-performing content
- Adjust next week's strategy
- Respond to any issues

Monthly (2 hours):

- Comprehensive performance analysis
- Strategy planning for next month
- Client or team reporting
- Tool and process optimization

Using Analytics to Improve Content

Content Performance Analysis:

1. **Identify Patterns**: What topics, formats, or posting times work best?
2. **Audience Insights**: Who is engaging with your content?
3. **Optimization Opportunities**: Where can you improve?
4. **Content Gaps**: What content is your audience asking for but not getting?

A/B Testing Framework:

- Test one variable at a time
- Run tests for at least 2 weeks
- Ensure statistical significance
- Document results for future reference

🎯 Action Item: Set Up Your Analytics System

Week 1: Install and configure all analytics tools

Week 2: Set up automated reporting

Week 3: Create your first baseline report

Week 4: Implement your monthly review process

Remember: Analytics are only valuable if they lead to action. Don't get lost in the data – use it to make better decisions.

Chapter 7: Scaling Your Social Media Presence

When to Hire Help vs. DIY

This is one of the most frequent questions I get: "Samridhi, when should I hire someone to help with social media?"

The answer isn't about follower count or revenue – it's about opportunity cost and expertise.

The DIY Phase (Months 1-6)

You should handle social media yourself when:

- You're just starting out and need to understand your audience
- Your budget is limited (under ₹25,000/month for marketing)
- You have fewer than 1,000 followers across all platforms
- You're still figuring out your brand voice and messaging
- You enjoy creating content and engaging with customers

DIY Success Requirements:

- Dedicate at least 1-2 hours daily to social media
- Invest in basic tools (scheduling, design, analytics)
- Commit to learning and staying updated
- Follow a structured approach (like our SPARK framework)

The Hybrid Phase (Months 6-12)

Consider getting part-time help when:

- You're spending more than 2 hours daily on social media
- Your business is growing and you need to focus on operations
- You're struggling with consistent content creation
- You want to expand to additional platforms
- Your social media is generating leads but you want to scale

Hybrid Approach Options:

- Virtual assistant for posting and basic engagement
- Freelance content creator for graphics and videos
- Part-time social media manager
- Social media management tools with automation

The Professional Phase (12+ Months)

It's time for professional help when:

- Social media is driving significant revenue (₹5+ lakhs/month)
- You want to run sophisticated ad campaigns
- You need to manage multiple platforms consistently
- You require advanced analytics and reporting
- You want to integrate social media with other marketing efforts

Building Your Social Media Team

Based on our experience at The Social Minder, here's how to build an effective social media team:

Small Business Team Structure (1-3 people):

- **Social Media Manager**: Strategy, content planning, community management (May charge 5-10k)
- **Content Creator**: Graphics, videos, photography (can be part-time). (May charge 5-10k)
- **Business Owner**: Brand voice, customer relationships, strategic decisions. (May charge 5-10k)

Growing Business Team Structure (3-5 people):

- **Social Media Strategist**: Overall strategy and planning (May charge 10-15k)
- **Content Creator**: Full-time content production (May charge 10-15k)
- **Community Manager**: Daily engagement and customer service. (May charge 10-15k)
- **Paid Ads Specialist**: Social media advertising (May charge 5-10k / 20 percent commission)
- **Analytics Specialist**: Performance tracking and optimization (May charge 10-15k)

The Social Minder Approach to Client Growth

Let me share our methodology for scaling clients' social media presence:

Phase 1: Foundation (Months 1-3)

Objectives: Establish presence, define brand voice, build initial audience

Activities:

- Complete platform optimization
- Develop content strategy and calendar
- Begin consistent posting schedule
- Establish engagement protocols
- Set up analytics and tracking

Success Metrics:

- Consistent posting schedule maintained
- Basic engagement established (comments, likes, shares)
- Website traffic from social media increasing
- Brand awareness growing in target market

Phase 2: Growth (Months 4-8)

Objectives: Scale content production, increase engagement, generate leads

Activities:

- Expand content types and formats
- Implement paid advertising campaigns
- Develop partnerships and collaborations
- Create lead magnets and opt-ins
- Optimize for conversions

Success Metrics:

- Follower growth rate of 15-25% monthly
- Engagement rate above industry average
- Consistent lead generation from social media
- Improved website conversion rates

Phase 3: Optimization (Months 9-12)

Objectives: Maximize ROI, scale successful strategies, expand reach

Activities:

- Advanced advertising campaigns
- Influencer partnerships
- User-generated content campaigns
- Marketing automation integration
- Advanced analytics implementation

Success Metrics:

- Social media contributing 20%+ of total leads
- Strong ROI on social media advertising
- High-quality leads with good conversion rates
- Brand recognition in target market

Hiring and Managing Social Media Team Members

What to Look for in a Social Media Manager:

- Understanding of your industry and target audience
- Strong writing and communication skills
- Experience with relevant platforms and tools
- Analytical mindset and data-driven approach
- Creativity and visual design sense
- Customer service orientation

Red Flags When Hiring:

- Promises of overnight success or viral content

- Focus only on follower growth, not business metrics
- Lack of industry-specific experience
- Poor communication or responsiveness
- No clear strategy or methodology
- Unwillingness to provide references or case studies

Managing Remote Social Media Teams

Most of our team at The Social Minder works remotely. Here's how we ensure quality and consistency:

Communication Protocols:

- Daily check-ins via Google Sheets
- Weekly strategy meetings via Google Meet
- Monthly performance reviews
- Quarterly planning sessions

Quality Control Systems:

- All content requires approval before posting
- Brand guidelines document for consistency
- Regular brand voice training sessions
- Performance monitoring and feedback

Tools for Team Collaboration:

- **WhatsApp & Sheets**: Daily communication and quick updates
- **Google Meet**: Video communication and training
- **Trello**: Project management and content planning

- **Google Drive**: File sharing and collaboration
- **Google Meet**: Team meetings and client calls

🎯 Action Item: Scaling Assessment

Evaluate your current situation:

Current Capacity Assessment:

1. How many hours per week do you spend on social media?
2. What tasks take the most time?
3. Which activities drive the best results?
4. What skills are you missing?

Growth Readiness Check:

1. Is social media generating consistent leads/sales?
2. Do you have budget for additional resources?
3. Are you ready to give up some control?
4. What are your growth goals for the next 12 months?

Resource Planning:

1. What's your budget for social media help?
2. Do you need full-time or part-time assistance?
3. What skills should you prioritize hiring?
4. How will you measure success of additional resources?

💡 Pro Tip: The Gradual Handoff Strategy

Don't try to hand off everything at once. Here's our recommended progression:

Week 1-2: New team member observes and learns

Week 3-4: They handle basic tasks (scheduling, responding to comments)

Week 5-8: They take on content creation with your approval

Week 9-12: They handle most tasks with periodic check-ins

Month 4+: They work independently with regular performance reviews

This ensures quality control while building confidence and competence.

Chapter 8: Troubleshooting Common Challenges

Real Questions from Real Clients

Over the years at The Social Minder, I've heard almost every social media challenge imaginable. Here are the most common ones and exactly how we solve them:

"My Posts Get No Engagement"

The Problem: You're posting consistently, but likes, comments, and shares are minimal.

Common Causes:

- Posting at wrong times for your audience
- Content doesn't provide value or spark emotion
- Not engaging with your audience first
- Using irrelevant or too many hashtags
- Poor quality visuals

The Social Minder Solution:

1. **Audit Your Posting Times**
    - Check your analytics for when your audience is most active
    - Test different posting times for 2 weeks
    - Use scheduling tools to post at optimal times
2. **Content Value Assessment**

    - Ask yourself: "Would I engage with this post if I weren't the business owner?"
    - Ensure every post provides education, entertainment, or inspiration
    - Add call-to-actions that encourage engagement
3. **Engagement First Strategy**
    - Spend 15 minutes before posting engaging with others' content
    - Respond to every comment on your posts within 2 hours
    - Ask questions in your captions

📊 **Client Example**: R's Restaurant was posting beautiful food photos but getting minimal engagement. We shifted to showing the cooking process, sharing recipes, and asking followers about their favorite dishes. Engagement increased by 80% in 30 days.

"I Don't Know What to Post"

The Problem: You stare at your phone or computer, completely blank on content ideas.

The Social Minder Content Generation System:

The 5-Bucket Method:

1. **Behind-the-Scenes** (30%): Your daily business operations
2. **Educational** (25%): Tips, how-tos, industry insights
3. **Customer-Focused** (20%): Reviews, testimonials, user content

4. **Personal** (15%): Your story, team, company culture
5. **Promotional** (10%): Products, services, offers

Content Inspiration Sources:

- Frequently asked questions from customers
- Industry news and trends
- Seasonal events and holidays
- Your business processes and behind-the-scenes
- Customer success stories
- Employee spotlights
- Local community events

🎯 **Action Item**: Create a "Content Ideas" note on your phone. Whenever something interesting happens in your business, add it to the list. As one of my professor - Mr. Sean Andrade at IIDE used to say, The Giant Balti. A content bucket that will help you during content block.

"Social Media Takes Too Much Time"

The Problem: You're spending hours daily on social media but not seeing proportional results.

Time Management Solutions:

Batch Content Creation:

- Dedicate 2-3 hours once per week to create all content
- Use templates for consistent formatting
- Repurpose content across multiple platforms
- Create content pillars for easy planning

Automation Without Losing Authenticity:

- Schedule posts in advance using Meta
- Set up Google Alerts for industry news to share
- Use templates for common responses
- Automate report generation

The 30-Minute Daily Routine:

- 10 minutes: Check notifications and respond to comments
- 10 minutes: Engage with others' content in your industry
- 10 minutes: Post or schedule next day's content

"I'm Not Getting Leads or Sales"

The Problem: Good engagement but it's not translating to business results.

Conversion Optimization Strategy:

1. **Optimize Your Profile**
    - Clear value proposition in bio
    - Link to specific landing page, not just homepage
    - Professional profile picture and cover image
    - Contact information easily accessible
2. **Create Clear Customer Journey**
    - Use Stories highlights to showcase services/products
    - Include clear call-to-actions in posts
    - Drive traffic to lead magnets (free guides, consultations)
    - Follow up with engaged users
3. **Track the Right Metrics**
    - Website traffic from social media
    - Email signups from social media
    - Consultation bookings
    - Direct messages inquiring about services

"My Competitors Are Doing Better"

The Problem: You see competitors with more followers, engagement, or apparent success.

Competitive Analysis Framework:

What to Analyze:

- Their posting frequency and times
- Content types that get most engagement
- How they interact with their audience
- Their promotional strategy

- Visual branding and consistency

What NOT to Copy:

- Their exact content or captions
- Their voice and personality
- Their promotional offers without adaptation
- Their posting schedule without testing

The Social Minder Competitive Strategy:

1. **Find Your Unique Angle**: What can you offer that they can't?
2. **Improve on Their Weaknesses**: Where are they falling short?
3. **Collaborate, Don't Compete**: Look for partnership opportunities
4. **Focus on Your Customers**: They know you better than competitors

"I Made a Social Media Mistake"

The Problem: You posted something inappropriate, made a typo, or received negative feedback.

Crisis Management Protocol:

For Minor Mistakes (typos, wrong information):

- Correct immediately with an edit or new post
- Acknowledge the mistake if it was significant
- Thank followers who pointed it out
- Learn and implement better review processes

For Major Issues (offensive content, customer complaints):

- Respond quickly but thoughtfully
- Take responsibility without making excuses
- Move detailed discussions to private messages
- Follow up publicly with resolution
- Review your content approval process

Prevention Strategies:

- Always review posts before publishing
- Have someone else review sensitive content
- Understand each platform's community guidelines
- Keep your brand voice guidelines handy

"I Can't Keep Up with Algorithm Changes"

The Problem: Every time you figure out a platform, the algorithm changes.

Algorithm-Proof Strategy:

Focus on Fundamentals:

- Create valuable, engaging content
- Build genuine relationships with your audience
- Encourage meaningful interactions
- Post consistently
- Use platform features as they're released

Stay Informed Without Obsessing:

- Follow 2-3 reliable social media news sources (Mosseri , Instagram)
- Join one professional community or group
- Test new features but don't abandon what works
- Focus on long-term relationship building

💡 **Pro Tip**: Algorithms favor engagement and relationships. If you focus on truly helping your audience, you'll succeed regardless of algorithm changes.

Emergency Response Strategies

When Things Go Really Wrong:

Negative Review Response:

1. Respond professionally and promptly
2. Acknowledge the concern
3. Offer to resolve privately
4. Follow up publicly when resolved
5. Learn and improve from feedback

Technical Issues:

1. Have backup posting methods ready
2. Communicate transparently with your audience
3. Use the downtime to plan future content
4. Don't panic – these issues are temporary

Team Member Mistakes:

1. Take responsibility as the business owner
2. Correct the mistake quickly
3. Review training and processes
4. Communicate changes to prevent recurrence

🎯 Quick Fixes Checklist

When things aren't working, run through this checklist:

Content Issues:

- [ ] Am I posting at optimal times?
- [ ] Is my content providing value?
- [ ] Am I using relevant hashtags?
- [ ] Are my visuals high quality?
- [ ] Do I include clear call-to-actions?

Engagement Issues:

- [ ] Am I responding to comments quickly?
- [ ] Do I engage with others' content?
- [ ] Am I asking questions in my posts?
- [ ] Is my content sparking conversation?

Business Results Issues:

- [ ] Is my profile optimized for conversions?
- [ ] Do I have clear next steps for interested followers?
- [ ] Am I tracking the right metrics?
- [ ] Have I set up proper lead capture systems?

Remember: Every social media challenge is an opportunity to improve and grow stronger.

Conclusion: Your 90-Day Action Plan

The Journey We've Taken Together

We've covered a lot of ground in this guide – from understanding the basics of social media marketing to scaling your presence and troubleshooting common challenges. But reading about strategies is just the first step. The real magic happens when you take action.

At The Social Minder, we've seen hundreds of small businesses transform their fortunes through strategic social media marketing. The difference between those who succeed and those who struggle isn't talent, budget, or luck – it's consistent, strategic action.

Your 90-Day Implementation Plan

Based on our experience working with clients, here's a proven 90-day plan to get you started:

Days 1-30: Foundation Phase

Week 1: Setup and Strategy

- [ ] Complete your platform audits and optimizations
- [ ] Define your target audience and brand voice
- [ ] Set up analytics tracking on all platforms
- [ ] Create your content pillars and themes
- [ ] Set realistic, measurable goals for 90 days

Week 2: Content Planning

- [ ] Create your first 30-day content calendar
- [ ] Batch create 2 weeks of content
- [ ] Set up scheduling tools
- [ ] Design content templates for consistency
- [ ] Plan your engagement strategy

Week 3: Launch and Optimize

- [ ] Begin posting according to your schedule
- [ ] Engage with your audience daily
- [ ] Monitor early performance metrics
- [ ] Adjust posting times based on engagement
- [ ] Refine your content based on early feedback

Week 4: Review and Refine

- [ ] Conduct your first monthly review
- [ ] Identify your best-performing content
- [ ] Adjust your strategy based on data
- [ ] Plan month 2 content calendar
- [ ] Celebrate your first month of consistent posting!

Days 31-60: Growth Phase

Week 5-6: Content Expansion

- [ ] Add new content types (video, live streaming, etc.)
- [ ] Experiment with different posting times
- [ ] Start engaging with industry peers and potential customers
- [ ] Launch your first lead magnet or special offer
- [ ] Begin building email list from social media traffic

Week 7-8: Community Building

- [ ] Focus on building genuine relationships
- [ ] Respond to every comment and message
- [ ] Share user-generated content
- [ ] Collaborate with complementary businesses
- [ ] Host your first Q&A or live session

Days 61-90: Optimization Phase

Week 9-10: Performance Analysis

- [ ] Conduct comprehensive 60-day review
- [ ] Identify your most effective strategies
- [ ] Calculate ROI on time and money invested
- [ ] Plan scaling strategies for successful tactics
- [ ] Consider additional platforms or team help

Week 11-12: Strategic Planning

- [ ] Set goals for your next 90 days
- [ ] Plan advanced strategies (paid ads, partnerships)
- [ ] Document your learnings and best practices
- [ ] Create systems for continued growth
- [ ] Celebrate your 90-day transformation!

Key Milestones to Track

30-Day Milestones:

- Consistent posting schedule established
- Basic engagement metrics improving
- Website traffic from social media increasing
- Clear brand voice developed

60-Day Milestones:

- Follower growth rate of 10-20%
- Regular engagement with your content
- First leads or inquiries from social media
- Improved website conversion rates

90-Day Milestones:

- Social media contributing to business goals
- Strong community of engaged followers
- Clear ROI on time and effort invested
- Sustainable systems and processes in place

Your Support System

Remember, you don't have to do this alone. Here are resources to help you succeed:

Free Resources:

- Platform-specific training from Facebook, Instagram, LinkedIn
- Industry blogs and newsletters
- YouTube tutorials and courses
- Local small business networking groups

Paid Resources:

- Social media management tools (Buffer, Hootsuite, Later)
- Design tools (Canva Pro, Adobe Creative Suite)
- Analytics tools (Sprout Social, Hootsuite Analytics)
- Online courses and certifications

Professional Help:

- Freelance content creators

- Social media virtual assistants
- Digital marketing consultants
- Agencies like The Social Minder

When to Get Professional Help

Consider professional help if:

- You're spending more than 15 hours/week on social media
- Your social media is generating significant revenue
- You want to scale faster than you can manage alone
- You need advanced strategies like paid advertising
- You're not seeing results after 6 months of consistent effort

Measuring Your Success

Don't just measure vanity metrics. Focus on:

Business Metrics:

- Website traffic from social media
- Leads generated through social media
- Revenue attributed to social media
- Customer acquisition cost from social media
- Customer lifetime value of social media customers

Engagement Quality:

- Comments and meaningful interactions
- Shares and saves of your content
- Direct messages and inquiries
- User-generated content featuring your business

- Brand mentions and referrals

The Long-Term Vision

Social media marketing isn't a sprint – it's a marathon. The businesses that succeed are those that commit to:

- **Consistency**: Showing up regularly for your audience
- **Authenticity**: Being genuine in all interactions
- **Value**: Always putting your audience's needs first
- **Patience**: Understanding that results take time
- **Learning**: Continuously improving and adapting

A Personal Message from Samridhi

As I write this conclusion, I'm reminded of why I started The Social Minder in the first place. I wanted to help small businesses like yours succeed in an increasingly digital world.

Social media marketing isn't about having the most followers or the viral post. It's about building genuine relationships with people who can benefit from your products or services. It's about creating a community around your brand and providing value consistently.

Every client who walks into The Social Minder office (or joins our Google calls) has a unique story, unique challenges, and unique opportunities. What unites them all is the desire to grow their business and serve their customers better.

You have something valuable to offer the world. Social media is simply a tool to help more people discover and benefit from what you do.

The strategies in this guide work – I've seen them transform businesses across industries and budgets. But they only work if you implement them consistently and authentically.

Your 90-day journey starts now. I believe in your success, and I'm excited to see what you'll achieve.

Here's to your social media success!

Samridhi Bhagat
Founder, The Social Minder

Bonus Resources

Content Templates

Instagram Caption Template:

Hook: [Attention-grabbing first line]
Value: [Main content/tip/story]
Call-to-Action: [What you want followers to do]
Hashtags: [Relevant hashtags for discovery]

Facebook Post Template:

Context: [Why this matters to your audience]
Content: [Main message/tip/announcement]

Engagement: [Question or call-to-action]

LinkedIn Post Template:

Personal Story: [Brief relevant experience]
Professional Insight: [Industry tip or observation]
Discussion Starter: [Question for engagement]

Essential Tools Checklist

Free Tools:

- [ ] Canva (design)
- [ ] Meta (scheduling)
- [ ] Google Analytics (tracking)
- [ ] Grammarly (copy editing)

Paid Tools (Recommended):

- [ ] Canva Pro ($12.99/month)
- [ ] Buffer Pro ($15/month)
- [ ] Hootsuite Professional ($49/month)
- [ ] Adobe Creative Suite ($52.99/month)
- [ ] Sprout Social ($99/month)

💡 Pro Tip: The Content Multiplication Strategy

Create one piece of core content and adapt it for multiple platforms:

1. **Start with a blog post** (1,000+ words)
2. **Create an infographic** summarizing key points

3. **Film a video** explaining the main concepts
4. **Extract quotes** for social media posts
5. **Create a podcast episode** discussing the topic
6. **Design Instagram carousel** with key takeaways
7. **Write LinkedIn article** with professional angle
8. **Create Twitter thread** with main points

This approach gives you 8+ pieces of content from one core idea.

30-Day Content Calendar Template

Week 1 - Getting Started

- Monday: Introduction post (who you are, what you do)
- Tuesday: Behind-the-scenes content
- Wednesday: Educational tip #1
- Thursday: Customer spotlight/testimonial
- Friday: Fun fact or industry insight
- Weekend: Personal story or team content

Week 2 - Building Value

- Monday: How-to tutorial
- Tuesday: Product/service showcase
- Wednesday: Educational tip #2
- Thursday: User-generated content
- Friday: FAQ response
- Weekend: Community appreciation

Week 3 - Engagement Focus

- Monday: Ask a question/poll

- Tuesday: Behind-the-scenes content
- Wednesday: Educational tip #3
- Thursday: Before/after transformation
- Friday: Industry news commentary
- Weekend: Team spotlight

Week 4 - Conversion Drive

- Monday: Case study/success story
- Tuesday: Special offer/promotion
- Wednesday: Educational tip #4
- Thursday: Customer testimonial
- Friday: Call-to-action post
- Weekend: Reflection/gratitude post

Crisis Management Checklist

When Something Goes Wrong:

- [ ] Don't panic - assess the situation calmly
- [ ] Respond quickly but thoughtfully
- [ ] Take responsibility when appropriate
- [ ] Move sensitive discussions to private messages
- [ ] Follow up publicly with resolution
- [ ] Document the incident and response
- [ ] Review processes to prevent recurrence
- [ ] Update crisis management procedures

Platform-Specific Best Practices

Instagram:

- Post 1-2 times daily
- Use 5-10 relevant hashtags
- Engage within first hour of posting

- Use Stories daily
- Create highlight reels for evergreen content

Facebook:

- Post 1-2 times daily
- Use native video when possible
- Engage with comments quickly
- Join relevant groups
- Use Facebook Live regularly

LinkedIn:

- Post 2-3 times per week
- Share industry insights
- Engage with others' content
- Publish long-form articles monthly
- Comment meaningfully on others' posts

YouTube:

- Upload consistently (weekly minimum)
- Optimize titles and descriptions
- Create custom thumbnails
- Engage with comments
- Use end screens and cards

Hashtag Research Guide

Instagram Hashtag Strategy:

- 30% broad hashtags (1M+ posts)
- 40% medium hashtags (100K-1M posts)
- 30% niche hashtags (10K-100K posts)

Hashtag Research Tools:

- Instagram's search function
- Hashtagify.me
- RiteTag
- Display Purposes
- All Hashtag

Final Thoughts

Thank you for taking this journey with me through "The Complete Guide to Social Media Marketing for Small Businesses." This guide represents years of experience, hundreds of client success stories, and thousands of hours of testing and refining strategies.

Remember these key principles:

1. **Start where you are** - You don't need to be perfect to begin
2. **Focus on value** - Always ask "What's in it for my audience?"
3. **Be consistent** - Small daily actions compound into big results
4. **Stay authentic** - Your personality is your competitive advantage
5. **Measure what matters** - Focus on metrics that impact your business
6. **Keep learning** - Social media is constantly evolving

Your next steps:

1. Choose your primary platforms (2-3 maximum to start)
2. Set up your analytics tracking
3. Create your first 30-day content calendar
4. Begin posting consistently
5. Engage with your audience daily
6. Review and optimize monthly

Join our community: We'd love to support you on your social media journey. Join The Social Minder community where small business owners share tips, celebrate wins, and support each other.

Share your success: We love hearing from readers who implement these strategies. Tag us @thesocialminder and share your wins – we celebrate every milestone with you!

Remember, every successful business started with a single post, a single follower, a single customer who believed in what they were building. Your story is just beginning.

Here's to your social media success!

The complete guide to transforming your small business through strategic social media marketing.

Contact Information

The Social Minder

Email: hello@thesocialminder.com

Website: www.thesocialminder.com

Phone: +919428917297

Samridhi Bhagat

LinkedIn: linkedin.com/in/samridhibhagat

Instagram: @thesocialminder

Email: thesocialminder.in@gmail.com

Connect with us for:

- Free 30-minute strategy consultation
- Custom social media audits
- Team training and workshops
- Done-for-you social media management
